AREA 51

AREA 51

ODYSSEYS

KEN KARST

CREATIVE EDUCATION · CREATIVE PAPERBACKS

Published by Creative Education and Creative Paperbacks
P.O. Box 227, Mankato, Minnesota 56002
Creative Education and Creative Paperbacks are imprints of
The Creative Company
www.thecreativecompany.us

Design by Blue Design; production by Colin O'Dea
Art direction by Rita Marshall
Printed in the United States of America

Photographs by Alamy (dotted zebra, RP Library, US
Air Force Photo, Len Wilcox, sandy young), Creative
Commons Wikimedia (Dallas Dispatch-Journal, FAS/
United States Geological Survey, NASA/GRIN), Dreamstime
(Abdullah AlSabahi), Getty Images (Jerod Harris/Getty
Images Entertainment, MATJAZ SLANIC/E+), iStockphoto
(ArisSu, BrianPIrwin, guvendemir, Gwengoat, Klubovy,
ktsimage, LPETTET, miroslav_1, mj0007, Opla, Redemption),
Shutterstock (andrea crisante, melhijad)

Library of Congress Cataloging-in-Publication Data
Names: Karst, Ken, author.
Title: Area 51 / Ken Karst.
Series: Odysseys in mysteries.
Includes index.
Summary: An in-depth study of Area 51, examining legends,
popular reports, and scientific evidence that supports or
refutes the mysterious phenomena reputed to occur there.
Identifiers: LCCN 2019049715 / ISBN 978-1-64026-359-8
(hardcover) / ISBN 978-1-62832-891-2 (pbk) / ISBN 978-1-
64000-513-6 (eBook)
Subjects: LCSH: Air bases—Nevada—Juvenile literature.
/ Unidentified flying objects—Juvenile literature. /
Extraterrestrial beings—Juvenile literature. / Area 51 (Nev.)—
Juvenile literature.
Classification: LCC TL789.2.K473 2021
DDC 358.4/170979314—dc23

First Edition HC 9 8 7 6 5 4 3 2 1
First Edition PBK 9 8 7 6 5 4 3 2 1

CONTENTS

Introduction

When Bob Lazar told a television reporter in 1989 that he'd been researching captured flying saucers at a United States military base in the Nevada desert, trying to figure out what made them fly so fast, "Area 51" suddenly became the key code name for government **conspiracies**. Bright lights and fast-moving objects had been regular features in the night sky above the restricted military zone north of Las Vegas since the 1950s,

OPPOSITE: People have many theories about what happens at Area 51, ranging from the study of alien technology to experiments in time travel.

causing many people to wonder what was going on out there. But those who worked in the zone were forbidden to tell anyone, even their spouses, what they did or saw.

The U.S. government, which controlled the land, refused to acknowledge the existence of any sort of base. Lazar believed such secrecy was standing in the way of greater scientific progress and broke his silence. Hearing stories from a scientist who claimed to have studied extraterrestrial technology confirmed many Americans' suspicions that beings from outer space had already visited Earth. People began to wonder about what the government was concealing and feared whatever beings could have been responsible for creating technology that seemed so advanced. Suddenly, Area 51 was on the map, in a big—but still invisible—way.

Can't Get There from Here

Area 51. It sounds like a railroad yard or a spot on a game board, not a legend like Shangri-La or Atlantis. But for more than half a century, Area 51 has been at the center of extraordinary American stories. Which of them are true? Which aren't?

One reason Area 51 has spun up so many vivid tales, perhaps, has to do with the fact that for decades, nearly everything about it was officially

OPPOSITE: Public access to Area 51 is blocked by fences, "No Trespassing" signs, and armed guards.

denied, or simply left unexplained. The *New York Times* once described it as "a base so secret it doesn't exist." And it's a well-known irony that secrecy often attracts the spotlight. But Area 51 does exist, and it has played a key role in American aeronautics, politics, and defense, even though its budget, operations, and employees have rarely been made public—sometimes not even to the president. When Lyndon B. Johnson took office in 1963 upon president John F. Kennedy's death, he had never heard of Area 51 and had no knowledge of a revolutionary spy plane that was being developed there. Area 51 has also been central to conspiracy theories and other scenarios involving military plots, government deception, cooperation with extraterrestrial beings, international intrigue, and fantastic technology.

It's easier to find Area 51 than it used to be, when

Physically, Area 51 is located about 100 miles (161 km) north of Las Vegas.

even U.S. Geological Survey maps didn't label it. Google Maps can take you right there and even show you runways, hangars, and other buildings—views that not long ago could have gotten you shot down if you were a pilot, arrested if you were hiking close enough to see them, or praised if you were a foreign spy. Physically, Area 51 is located about 100 miles (161 km) north of Las Vegas. It's in barren, desert terrain, an area of dry lakebeds and low mountains, creosote bushes and Joshua trees. The base is surrounded by the Nevada Test and Training Range (NTTR), a nearly 5,000-square-mile (12,950 sq km) piece of the Nevada desert as big as the state of Connecticut.

It also abuts the U.S. Department of Energy's Nevada National Security Site (NNSS), a 1,360-square-mile (3,522 sq km) area where nearly 1,000 nuclear weapons were tested from the 1950s through the 1990s. Area 51 itself covers about 600 square miles (1,554 sq km) and is heavily guarded both on and above the ground. Even air force pilots from the NTTR are forbidden from flying into the airspace above Area 51; those who cut even a corner are escorted to the ground by fighter jets and interrogated. On the ground, security cameras and motion detectors ring the site. Hikers encounter signs telling them that the use of deadly force is authorized to keep them out, and are often quickly met by security guards in vehicles. No one knows exactly what entity employs the guards, who wear camouflage and thus are known casually as "camo dudes."

rea 51 most likely got its name from the scheme that was used to name sections of the NTTR. The range is divided into nearly 30 numbered areas, 1 through 30. But there are no areas numbered 31 through 50. Some people think Area 51 may have gotten its name because it is next to Area 15, but no one is sure. Over the years, officials and pilots have called it "Watertown," "Paradise Ranch," "The Box," and "Dreamland."

Why put an important military operation out in the desert? In the 1930s, that part of the Nevada desert was a wild country, far from any towns or people and home to deer and wild horses. In the 1950s, president Dwight D. Eisenhower ordered the development of a plane that could fly—so high that it could not be shot down—over the Soviet Union to look at military bases. A top-secret

site was needed. The project director, an economist and professor named Richard Bissell, who had been ambassador to the Soviet Union after World War II, flew all over the west in a small plane with Herbert Miller, a Central Intelligence Agency (CIA) expert on Soviet nuclear capabilities, and Kelly Johnson, director of the high-performance plane development division for the Lockheed Martin Corporation, in search of a site. They visited Nevada's Groom Lake, a salt flat that was as smooth and hard as a runway and also neighbored the NTTR. The area was perfect.

Within months, the Groom Lake site became the training area for the U-2 spy plane, one of the most notorious U.S. aircraft ever launched. The planes were built in Burbank, California, disassembled, and loaded onto air force transport planes. Pilots carrying the parts

Area 51 was cleared of people in 1957 after the Hood bomb, a 74-kiloton nuclear bomb was detonated at a test nearby.

took off not knowing what their destination was, only that they would receive instructions on the way. When they had descended to hundreds of feet above the ground, into what looked like utter darkness, the Area 51 runway lights flashed on and guided them in. Moments after they landed, the lights shut off again.

Though it quickly became a key part of U.S. defense activities, Area 51 was cleared of people in 1957 after the Hood bomb, a 74-kiloton nuclear bomb, was detonated at a test nearby, saturating the area with plutonium, a radioactive material deadly to humans. The Hood bomb was six times more powerful than those dropped on

A Good Guess

The U.S. Air Force designed its F-117 Nighthawk to avoid **radar** detection, but a plastic model turned out to be anything but invisible to consumers. A designer for Testor Corporation, John Andrews, used publicly available information—filling in gaps with his own understanding of military aircraft—to design a model of the stealth fighter he guessed the air force was building at Area 51 in the early 1980s. Testor unveiled its F-19 Stealth Fighter model in 1986, and although—or perhaps *because*—the air force refused to acknowledge the plane existed, Testor soon sold more than 700,000 of the models, making it the most popular aircraft model ever. Once the F-117 was publicly revealed two years later, people realized that the model was very different from the real thing. Still, the popularity of the model and the refusal by the air force to acknowledge anything about the real plane prompted hearings to be held in Congress, an example of how secrecy can work against itself. Andrews regarded models as teaching tools, and although he was an army veteran, he was also critical of the government for concealing information from its own citizens. He died in 1999.

Area 51 remained closed and deserted until January 1960, when the air force began designing a plane invisible to radar that would fly higher and faster than the U-2.

Hiroshima and Nagasaki, Japan, in 1945. It is still the largest nuclear bomb ever to have been detonated over the continental U.S. Area 51 remained closed and deserted until January 1960, when the air force began designing a plane invisible to radar that would fly higher and faster than the U-2. The Area 51 runway was extended to nearly 6 miles (9.7 km) in length, and the restricted airspace above it was expanded from 50 square miles (129 sq km) to 440 square miles (1,140 sq km). That allowed for development of the Archangel 12, known more simply as the A-12; and later the SR-71 Blackbird, which flew in the Persian Gulf War of the early 1990s; and the F-117 Nighthawk, a dominant player in the Persian Gulf War as well as in the War on Terror.

Such engineering developments made Area 51 a busy place, although it remained remote and inhospitable. The area is still windy and dusty, with temperatures that can fluctuate from 100 °F (37.8 °C) on summer days to 0 °F (-17.8 °C) on winter nights, with daily temperature swings of 40 degrees considered normal. Yet the air force, CIA, and Lockheed ultimately installed barracks, dining halls, and other amenities for hundreds of workers, whom they flew to Area 51 weekly from Las Vegas on commercial jets with covered windows. On the ground, workers were often shuttled from place to place on buses, also with blacked-out windows.

It wasn't until 1978 that the city of Rachel, Nevada,

was established along Route 375 about 25 miles (40.2 km) outside the east gate of Area 51, giving official status to the ramshackle collection of homes for about 100 people. Rachel was as close as anyone without high-level security clearance or a sturdy vehicle could get to Area 51, so over time it attracted a steady stream of people curious about secret aircraft, lights in the night sky, sonic booms, and what seemed to be a concentration of unidentified flying objects (UFOs). And after Bob Lazar's interviews in the late 1980s, the small town became internationally known.

A Man-made Mystery

Area 51 has always placed a premium on secrecy. As a project developed in part by the CIA, the lead U.S. intelligence-gathering agency, the site's concealment was of top importance. The remote desert location aided that effort, but the secrecy went much farther. Employees and even supervisors were often not told what their work was about or how it related to work others were doing,

OPPOSITE: Before World War II, the area near Groom Lake was used for mining silver and lead.

and they were forbidden from discussing it. Even in the 1980s, after the workforce had swelled to a reported 2,000 people (which would have placed it among Nevada's 20 largest cities, had the workers lived there), employees had to sign confidentiality pledges stating that they would not discuss their work or even their workplace with anybody, under penalty of 10 years in prison or a $10,000 fine.

As a result, the work at Area 51 became known as "black projects," their cost and purpose concealed even from Congress. (Reports indicated that the Area 51 budget reached about $1 billion per year.) When an A-12 from Area 51 crashed in Utah in 1963 and a vacationing family came upon the wreckage, CIA officials who had pursued the aircraft confiscated film from the family's camera and paid them off in cash. Similarly, in 1962, when a Greyhound bus scraped against a trailer

The work at Area 51 became known as "black projects," their cost and purpose concealed even from Congress.

carrying parts of an A-12 to Area 51, officials quickly and quietly authorized payment of $5,000 for damages to the bus to prevent an insurance claim or any other kind of legal process.

When some workers who had developed diseases they believed to have been caused by the burning of toxic materials at Area 51 (not even the trash was allowed to be carried out, so everything was destroyed on site), they went to court in 1994 to discover the truth. The government sealed all records related to the case, even those of the workers' lawyer, preventing the public from seeing them. The government even refused to admit whether there was jet fuel or paint on the site. President Bill Clinton then exempted Area 51 from Environmental Protection Agency (EPA) requirements that inventories of hazardous waste be made public, and in 1998, the courts ruled that the trial could not continue, since the government would not provide key information. Though Area 51's special exemption was renewed every year since then, the case cracked the walls of secrecy around Area 51. The government finally acknowledged in the court proceedings that it had "an operating location near Groom Lake." But that was all.

Area 51 may have been shrouded in secrecy to prevent other nations from learning about American military technology, but this secrecy had a peculiar effect on the U.S. itself. In 1947, shortly after the end of World War II, when international relations were tense and uncertain,

According to a CIA report released in 1997, the agency had investigated nearly 1,000 UFO reports by 1951.

there was a mysterious aircraft crash in the desert outside Roswell, New Mexico. First described even by the U.S. Army as a flying saucer—an account that was amended within a day—the occurrence was part of a wave of UFO reports that endured for several years.

According to a CIA report released in 1997, the agency had investigated nearly 1,000 UFO reports by 1951, often interviewing citizen-witnesses but swearing them to secrecy. Faced with a public that seemed convinced that UFOs had come from elsewhere in the universe, guided by intelligent beings using sophisticated technology, the government was in a delicate spot. If aliens really had landed, apparently without warning, could the government tell the public that they had? Wouldn't people begin to doubt the government's defense systems? If any extraterrestrials had survived, where were they? Were they in our midst, somehow? One idea that emerged was that extraterrestrials had come to take human organs because their own were failing. According to the theory, the government and the outer-space visitors had struck a deal: the visitors could capture humans and extract certain organs, while the government would learn from the extraterrestrials how to build aircraft like theirs—extremely fast, capable of hovering and darting from side to side, and able to accelerate with unimaginable quickness. So if the government was engaged in developing sophisticated aircraft at Area 51, it stood to reason (to some) that aliens were also being held there. And that

The Cold War

At the end of World War II, the former Allied powers—the United States, Great Britain, and the Soviet Union—disagreed on how to rebuild Europe. The Soviet Union wanted to control its neighbors and spread communism. The U.S. and Great Britain wanted to establish capitalist, **democratic** states in places that had been destroyed during the war. All had seen the destructive power of the world's first atomic bomb, dropped by the U.S. over Japan in 1945, and understood the dangerous potential of that technology. But the nations were also at odds. So they resorted to a new way of fighting: the Cold War. It was a conflict in which, for nearly 50 years, the U.S. and Soviet Union spent billions building and testing weapons but not using them against one another, for fear of triggering nuclear retaliation. Political tensions forced many nations to choose sides and fueled actual wars in places such as Korea and Vietnam. And, of course, the Cold War made spying into an international industry, supported by secrecy. That directly contributed to the development of Area 51 as a test site for groundbreaking aircraft. Without Cold War espionage, Area 51 may never have existed.

seemed to explain the secrecy.

The U.S. citizenry had been carried away by UFO dramas in the past—most notably in 1938, when a dramatic radio broadcast based on the novel *War of the Worlds* caused a national panic and led people to believe Earth had been invaded by aliens who had landed in New Jersey. Reaction to the broadcast, which was designed to mimic a series of news bulletins, was intense enough that phone lines in some cities were overloaded with callers checking with neighbors and family members. For a time in the early 1960s, the CIA was concerned that a similar hoax could divert the nation's air defense system so thoroughly that the U.S. would be vulnerable to an air assault from a real enemy, such as the Soviet Union. For a while, the air force cooperated with ufologists, but in *Area 51: An Uncensored History of America's Top*

A series of governmental commissions through the 1950s and '60s determined that UFOs were not real, and some accounts assert that this caused the press to lose interest in the subject.

Secret Military Base, author Annie Jacobsen asserts that such teamwork simply allowed the CIA to investigate people who had collected vast amounts of information about UFOs and find out what they knew.

A series of governmental commissions through the 1950s and '60s determined that UFOs were not real, and some accounts assert that this caused the press to lose interest in the subject. Against this backdrop, Area 51's secret expansion continued well into the 1980s. Some historians argue that there were two reasons why the government was willing to allow UFOs to be the subject of public controversy: The first was that the attention encouraged support for anything that looked like the government's investigation into the mystery, even though governmental commissions tended to dismiss the notion of UFOs. The second was that speculation about UFOs diverted attention from the development and testing of very real aeronautical breakthroughs at Area 51, such as the U-2 and other spy and fighter planes.

Despite scientific attempts to debunk UFOs, sightings continued. In the 1980s, sightings of black triangles in the sky above Belgium caused a stir. In 1975, radar over the U.S. and Canada tracked the most UFOs ever in a single wave, but the North American Aerospace Defense Command (NORAD, the same institution that every December tracks the whereabouts of another mysterious figure: Santa Claus) said aircraft in the corresponding areas failed to confirm a single one. Through the years, some scholars have suggested that uncertainties about UFOs might be more important than official sources acknowledge. In 1966, a group of scientists determined that 15 percent of UFO sightings could not be explained as planes, weather balloons, atmospheric gas, or other common occurrences—a far higher share than the 9 percent a government inquiry found. As far back as 1960, the Brookings Institution declared that, while the discovery of intelligent life elsewhere in the universe was "not likely," it also "could happen at any time." So what were those hovering, darting, intensely bright lights people kept seeing above Area 51?

Folks and Fiction

Legends surround Bob Lazar. Most of
them were of his own making, outlined
in several interviews in 1989, in which
he tore off the cloak of secrecy
regarding UFO landings and aliens
that had surrounded Area 51 for nearly
40 years. In the early 1980s, Lazar
was operating a successful business
out of his Las Vegas home, processing
photographic film for real estate
appraisers. What was perhaps more
notable, though, was that Lazar

OPPOSITE: Bob Lazar claimed that he once worked with alien
technology, including fuel, at Area 51.

delivered the processed film in a jet-powered car he had designed himself.

Around the same time, Lazar, who claimed to have earned master's degrees in electronic technology from the California Institute of Technology and physics from the Massachusetts Institute of Technology, was attending a conference where he spotted Edward Teller, known as the "Father of the Hydrogen Bomb." Teller was reading an article about Lazar and his car. Lazar introduced himself, and Teller later invited him to come to work on a project in Nevada involving aircraft.

Lazar signed an oath swearing he'd never reveal what he was working on and agreed to have his phone tapped and his car and home searched without warning. He was flown to a base north of Las Vegas and taken in a bus with blacked-out windows to a facility where he

Lazar introduced himself, and Teller later invited him to come to work on a project in Nevada involving aircraft.

saw a large, disk-shaped craft with tiny seats in a hangar. He was then taken to a room, handed a large stack of material to study, and left alone. When his escort closed the door, Lazar noticed a poster on the back of the door that showed a picture of a dry lakebed with a saucer-like aircraft and the words "They're here."

Over time, Lazar saw or read reports about nine crafts and determined the vehicles had been fueled by Element 115, a substance he theorized could have unique gravitational properties as it decayed, thus allowing aircraft to travel great distances. He also claimed to have read autopsy reports of bodies that had been in the aircraft, referring to them as "The Kids" and describing them as short and hairless, with large heads and almond-shaped eyes. He even glimpsed a living one through the window of a room as he was being ushered past. Lazar studied documents stating that the spacecraft had come from Zeta Reticuli, a binary star system 200 trillion miles (322 trillion km) away. Several years earlier, a husband and wife who claimed they'd been abducted by aliens had said their abductors had come from Zeta Reticuli.

Lazar had come to believe that what had already been learned at Area 51 needed the involvement of more scientists, not secrecy. "Just the concept that there's definite proof, and we can even have articles from another world, another system ... you can't just not tell everyone," Lazar said.

When Lazar was caught with several friends trying

to get a closer look at Area 51, he was fired. A short time later he gave his first interview on Las Vegas television in a way that concealed his identity. But after he was run off the highway and shot at in his car by people he believed were trying to protect Area 51's secrecy, he decided to reveal himself on television as a safeguard. He quickly became a folk hero to ufologists. However, his story was undermined when the universities he claimed to have attended reported they had no records of him. Lazar said the government had stolen the evidence and even destroyed his birth certificate, but the damage to his reputation was done.

Like Lazar, Glenn Campbell called himself a "lobbyist for openness." Campbell, who had made some money designing a computer program for banks, moved from Boston, Massachusetts, to Rachel, Nevada, in 1993 after the air force expanded the restricted area surrounding Area 51. Working in a bar-restaurant in the desert outpost and calling himself "Psychospy," Campbell set up the organizations called Secrecy Oversight Council and Whitesides Defense Committee (named for nearby Whitesides Mountain, which for years had offered an overlook of Area 51 before the air force declared it off-limits). He published his own document (*The Area 51 Viewers' Guide*), advised the growing number of visitors on their rights and the proper responses if confronted by security agents when venturing near Area 51, and posted a regular online newsletter called "The Groom Lake Desert Rat" that covered a wide-ranging compendium of news, science, speculation, policy, and politics. Campbell called the trailer he moved into the "Area 51 Research Center." He explored and marked a route to an overlook

Saucers: Keep Left

Nevada Route 375 carries the usual traffic—cars, trucks, and motorcycles—through nearly 100 miles (161 km) of desert from Ash Springs to Warm Springs. But could some of those headlights belong to vehicles of unknown origin? Possibly, since the road has been officially designated as the Extraterrestrial Highway. The road runs within about 25 miles (40.2 km) of Area 51, closer than any other major thoroughfare to the site long rumored to be a place where researchers were working with captured UFOs and aliens. The designation accompanied the promotion of the 1996 film *Independence Day*, in which Area 51 is a key location. When the Nevada legislature nixed the highway name change, governor Bob Miller got the state transportation board to authorize it anyway. The dedication of the highway, held at the Little A'Le'Inn in Rachel, Nevada, was attended by numerous movie stars and a person claiming to represent the "intergalactic tourism association." Still one of the least-traveled roads in Nevada, the highway is now posted with signs showing pictures of flying saucers. Even though it passes through wide-open, lonely country, drivers still have to watch how fast they're going. The speed limit is Warp 7.

Campbell was ... the opposite of Lazar.... He didn't believe in aliens.

just outside Area 51 that he named "Freedom Ridge." In 1994, he took a Nevada state legislator up Freedom Ridge to show him how the activity and development at Area 51 proved the air force hadn't been paying enough property taxes to surrounding Lincoln County. Campbell also published the radio frequencies that the Area 51 security guards used, as well as arrival and departure times for planes carrying workers from and to Las Vegas.

Campbell was in some ways the opposite of Lazar and the people who came to Rachel to get close to Area 51 and perhaps connect with aliens. He didn't believe in aliens. His *Viewers' Guide* warns people that the most dangerous creatures they might encounter are not aliens or security patrols but cows. In an interview with author

David Darlington for his book *Area 51: The Dreamland Chronicles*, Campbell said the community of UFO followers "is full of nuts and ridiculous folklore" and that UFO sightings are examples of people's imaginations at work. "When people look at a light in the sky, what they see indicates something about what's inside of them," he said. "I'm not into UFOs," he said. "I'm into humanity and philosophy."

Lazar and Campbell were part of an eccentric band of Area 51 monitors that occasionally put the town of Rachel in the national news. But they couldn't have done it without reports of UFOs and extraterrestrials.

Underlying Area 51's mystery is the notion that it is the place where the remains of the 1947 Roswell crash are being kept, examined, and perhaps duplicated. That possibility has sparked the imaginations not only of ufologists but also of the Nevada tourism industry, Hollywood, and other generators of American popular culture.

The 2008 Indiana Jones movie *The Kingdom of the Crystal Skull* expanded the mystery even further by suggesting that the remains of the Ark of the Covenant were stored at Area 51. Several aspects of Lazar's story—such as Zeta Reticuli and Element 115—were key features of the television series *Seven Days*, which dealt with a time-traveling spacecraft developed from remains of the crashed Roswell craft. The 1996 film *Independence Day* used Area 51 as the place where the president was taken to hide from attacking aliens and where the Roswell remains were used to repel the attack and ultimately save the world from annihilation. A 2005 video game, *Area 51*, is built on the notion of aliens trading their technological know-how for human test subjects who would provide them with a virus to use in a war in their home world. And some who argue that the 1969 Apollo moon landing was a hoax say it was all filmed at Area 51.

The television series *The X-Files* located one of its episodes in Rachel, Nevada, outside of Area 51. In real life, Rachel has styled itself as "The UFO Capital of the World." In 2006, the town received publicity when KFC installed an 87,500-square-foot (8,129 sq m) tile version of its logo on the desert floor at the edge of Rachel, announcing that it would be the only business logo visible from space. (The company removed it in 2007.) Meanwhile, Rachel has become a draw for geocachers, thanks to the 1,500 geocaches placed along Route 375, the "Extraterrestrial Highway," in 2011.

Straight Stories, Stranger Stories

Some of the cloud of mystery around Area 51 has evaporated in recent years. Details of the U-2 project were **declassified** in 1998, allowing it to be known—more than 40 years after the fact—that pilot Ray Goudey had been the first man to fly a plane higher than 65,000 feet (19,812 m).

In 2007, decades after workers at Area 51 hustled the A-12 into a hangar several times a day to keep it from being viewed by satellites, the CIA displayed an A-12 in front of its Langley, Virginia, headquarters, as part of the agency's 60th anniversary celebration. The public was allowed to stroll by the titanium-skinned aircraft that could fly up to an altitude of 90,000 feet (27,432 m) at 3 times the speed of sound. It was still the only plane capable of flying that high and that fast. Before the 1964 presidential election, President Johnson, eager to illustrate American progress on defense technology, wanted to make the A-12 public. An aide told him it was for "strategic reconnaissance." Johnson, apparently latching onto the first letter of each of those words, made a public revelation about a new spy plane called the SR-71. The SR-71 Blackbird thus got all the press attention, while the CIA's A-12 was able to remain a secret. The A-12 has rarely been seen in flight, although it is believed

that many reported UFO sightings have actually been extremely fast and highly reflective A-12s.

I n the early days of stealth technology, the Blackbird was groundbreaking. The design of the aircraft used angled surfaces and materials that absorbed radar beams rather than reflecting them and allowing the planes to be tracked. On radar, the 107-foot-long (32.6 m) Blackbird, with a wingspan of nearly 58 feet (17.7 m), appeared to have an area of 108 square feet (10 sq m). Thirty-two SR-71s were built, and most had long careers: the air force flew them from 1964 to 1998. But

The F-117 Nighthawk was 66 feet (20.1 m) long with a wingspan of 43 feet (13.1 m), but the bat-shaped aircraft appeared on radar to be the size of a ball bearing.

designers and air force officials felt the plane, or at least its radar image, was still too big. The air force's F-117 Nighthawk (active from 1981 to 2008) represented a vast improvement in radar-evasion technology. Although it was 66 feet (20.1 m) long with a wingspan of 43 feet (13.1 m), the bat-shaped aircraft appeared on radar to be the size of a ball bearing! Area 51 might have needed secrecy to operate initially, but by the 1980s it was producing secrecy itself, in a way.

For many years, aviation buffs and ufologists had asserted that a plane called the Aurora, capable of flying at five times the speed of sound, was under development at Area 51. That is still largely regarded as legend. But in the meantime, Area 51 saw the development of an even newer concept in aircraft: unmanned flights.

Drone technology—flying aircraft by remote control—was first used in World War II, though it did not meet with great success then. In fact, the older brother of President Kennedy was killed in 1944 when a bomber from which he was supposed to eject (allowing it to be guided to its target by another plane nearby) exploded over Germany. But the CIA continued to pursue the idea, producing the Predator drone in the 1990s for reconnaissance purposes.

By 2000, concerned about the activities of al Qaeda terrorist Osama bin Laden, the CIA outfitted the Predator with Hellfire missiles, and, for training, built a mockup of bin Laden's compound in Afghanistan on the edge

Roswell

Accounts of flying objects carrying strange visitors go back thousands of years. But the modern UFO era can be traced to 1946, perhaps because World War II, which had featured extensive combat in the air, brought new awareness of the dangers the skies could bring. In 1946 alone, there was a six-week wave of UFO sightings in the Pacific Northwest. But the next year, a crash near Roswell, New Mexico, was a game-changer. An army information officer put out a news release saying a saucer had crashed, and the news went international. The next day, the army took back that statement and claimed the object had been a weather balloon. In the 1990s, the air force said the debris had come from a device designed to detect Soviet nuclear tests, but by then "Roswell" had become synonymous with tales of alien visitors to Earth and associated government cover-ups. Roswell's reputation also involved Area 51, situated nearly 1,000 miles (1,609 km) west. According to the story, whatever crashed near Roswell, including live alien crew members, was taken to Wright-Patterson Air Force Base in Ohio—some say by tunnel, though it's 2,000 miles (3,219 km) away—and then removed to Area 51 for further research.

TAKEAWAY

In August 2013, the government officially acknowledged the existence of Area 51 by declassifying a 1992 CIA report.

of Area 51. Drone reconnaissance and missiles enabled the CIA to kill al Qaeda operative Qaed Salim Sinan al-Harethi in the desert of Yemen in 2002. Ten years later, according to reports, Predators flying in the Middle East were being operated by "pilots" at computers just outside Area 51.

In August 2013, the government officially acknowledged the existence of Area 51 by declassifying a 1992 CIA report. Some believed the move indicated the government was becoming less secretive, while others wondered if the news was meant to prepare the public for the truth about alien activities. In nearby Rachel,

declassifications have enabled former A-12 workers to meet in reunions, some at the Little A'Le'Inn. Even former CIA staffers show up. Some formed a group called Roadrunners Internationale. Its purpose is to preserve the history of Area 51 and the people who worked there on some of history's most influential aircraft. The group's website provides details on equipment, training, and who flew what planes how often, as well as photographs and a list of where the remaining A-12s can now be seen. Reunions are often covered by news media but also have the flavor of a meeting of any business or alumni association. Members swap stories, play golf, and sell memorabilia—including the only official CIA material allowed for sale outside CIA headquarters at Langley.

Declassification has also provided dramatic twists to the tales that have long surrounded Area 51. In her 2011

The pupose of Roadrunners Internationale is to preserve the history of Area 51 and the people who worked there on some of history's most influential aircraft.

book, Annie Jacobsen reports that the disks that crashed at Roswell in 1947 were most definitely not from another planet. They were from the Soviet Union—a fact that could be determined from the Cyrillic writing inside the craft. The Soviets apparently had exploited disk-flight technology developed by German Nazis whom they had either captured or were still in contact with after World War II. But then the book makes an even more dramatic assertion. Quoting an unnamed engineer who worked on the remains of the crash, Jacobsen writes that the creatures in the craft were human children, whose large heads and strange eyes were in fact examples of human experimentation performed by Nazis during and after World War II, under an agreement between the Nazis and Soviet dictator Joseph Stalin. Stalin, the engineer was told, believed that by sending the small aviators in a disk to crash in the U.S., he could cause a panic in the country that the government might be unable to handle. Area 51 workers who were extensively quoted elsewhere in the book said after it was published that they were unaware of any such things happening at Area 51 and were shocked to read about them.

These days, the town of Rachel is quieter than it used to be. After the air force expanded the secure zone around Area 51 in 1995 to include Freedom Ridge, Glenn Campbell, founder of the Area 51 Research Center, left. The center closed several years later. One of the few remaining operational businesses in Rachel is the Little

A'Le'Inn ("Earthlings Welcome!"), home of the "Alien Burger." On the restaurant's website, owner Pat Travis sums up why she's still there: "Life is a mystery. Enjoy the ride." Indeed, no matter how many documents are declassified or how many reports of UFOs are debunked, Area 51 will continue to draw people seeking contact with other worlds and eager to probe the mysteries that surround the base.

Selected Bibliography

Campbell, Glenn. *Area 51 Viewer's Guide*. Rachel, Nev.: Area 51 Research Center, 1995.

Darlington, David. *Area 51: The Dreamland Chronicles; the Legend of America's Most Secret Military Base*. New York: Henry Holt, 1997.

Hansen, Terry. "The Psychology of Dreamland: How Secrecy is Destroying Public Faith in Government and Science." *AboveTopSecret.com*. http://www.abovetopsecret.com/forum/thread60181/pg1.

Jacobsen, Annie. *Area 51: An Uncensored History of America's Top Secret Military Base*. New York: Little, Brown, 2011.

Patton, Phil. *Dreamland: Travels Inside the Secret World of Roswell and Area 51*. New York: Villard, 1998.

Rich, Ben, and Leo Janos. *Skunk Works: A Personal Memoir of My Years at Lockheed*. New York: Little, Brown, 1994.

Wright, Susan. *UFO Headquarters: Investigations on Current Extraterrestrial Activity*. New York: St. Martin's Press, 1998.

Endnotes

aeronautics the study or practice of aircraft navigation

altitude the vertical elevation, or height of an object or point in relation to sea level or ground level

autopsy an examination of a dead body to determine the cause of death

binary having two parts

budget the amount of money required to operate a household, office, government, or other enterprise; government budgets are usually renewed yearly or every other year

conspiracies secret plans, involving several or many participants, to accomplish something unlawful or harmful

Cyrillic an alphabet derived from the Greek alphabet and used for Slavic languages, including Russian

debunk prove false

declassified opened to the public; no longer secret

democratic controlled by the people; a form of government featuring majority rule

economist an expert in economics, the wealth and resources of a place

element a substance that cannot be broken down into simpler components

extraterrestrial describing a being or object from beyond Earth

geocachers	people who, for recreation, find items hidden in the landscape by using global positioning devices
gravitational	having to do with gravity, the force that pulls bodies toward one another
hoax	a humorous or harmful deception; a trick
intelligence	information having military, political, or other strategic value
irony	the occurrence of the opposite of what might be expected
kiloton	an explosive force equivalent to 1,000 metric tons of TNT
radar	a system used to detect objects such as aircraft and determine their position and velocity, derived from the words "radio detection and ranging"
radioactive	emitting ionizing radiation or particles
reconnaissance	a search for useful military information
security clearance	permission to enter guarded places or read certain secret material
sonic booms	explosive sounds made by the compression of sound waves as an object moves at the speed of sound
terrain	a stretch of land and its physical features
ufologists	people who study reports, recordings, and other evidence related to UFOs

World War II a worldwide conflict that involved more than 70 nations; the war was instigated by German dictator Adolf Hitler in 1939 and ended in 1945 with the defeat of Germany, Italy and Japan.

Websites

Area 51
http://www.ufomind.com/area51/

Area 51 history, geography, corporate and military connections, photos, news articles, and back issues of "The Desert Rat" newsletter.

Secret Heroes
http://area51specialprojects.com/

History, photos, biographies, and personal accounts of Area 51 from people who worked there.

Note: Every effort has been made to ensure that any websites listed above were active at the time of publication. However, because of the nature of the Internet, it is impossible to guarantee that these sites will remain active indefinitely or that their contents will not be altered.

Index